GEOGRAPHICS

HUMANS

RESEARCHED AND WRITTEN BY
SUSAN MARTINEAU

DESIGNED AND ILLUSTRATED BY
VICKY BARKER

www.bsmall.co.uk

Published by b small publishing ltd. www.   • 1 2 3 4 5 • ISBN 978-1-911509-87-5
Pro   o. Ltd.

HELLO PEOPLE!

Scientists think that there have been creatures like humans on the planet for two million years. But the first humans who were most like us are called *Homo sapiens*. This means 'wise man' in Latin. Once they began to explore the world there was no stopping them – or us!

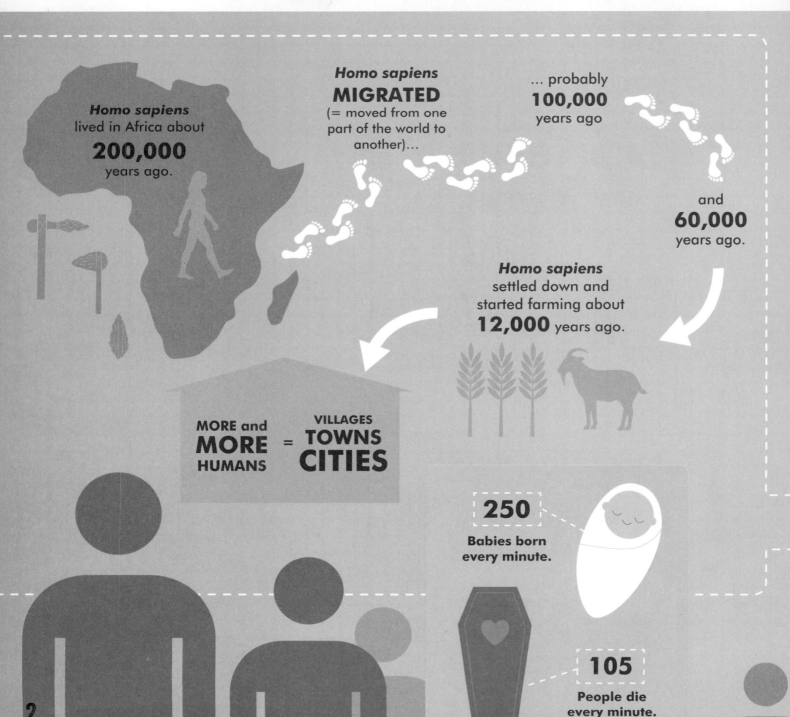

Homo sapiens lived in Africa about **200,000** years ago.

Homo sapiens **MIGRATED** (= moved from one part of the world to another)...

... probably **100,000** years ago

and **60,000** years ago.

Homo sapiens settled down and started farming about **12,000** years ago.

MORE and **MORE** HUMANS = VILLAGES **TOWNS CITIES**

250 Babies born every minute.

105 People die every minute.

HUMANS AT WORK

ARCHAEOLOGISTS look at ancient objects, bones and buildings to find out how people lived in the past. They are like history detectives.

 There are more Lego people in the world than real ones!

BILLIONS OF US!

11 BILLION
PREDICTED BY 2100

?

1 BILLION
1804
World's first locomotive pulled a train.

2 BILLION
1930
First ever Football World Cup.

3 BILLION
1960
First laser was built.

4 BILLION
1974
Rubik's Cube was invented.

5 BILLION
1987
800,000 people celebrated 50th anniversary of Golden Gate Bridge in San Francisco, USA.

6 BILLION
1999
Bertrand Piccard and Brian Jones went non-stop around the world in a hot air balloon.

7 BILLION
2011
First artificial organ transplant.

+

WHERE WE LIVE

We are so lucky to have such a beautiful planet to live on. Humans make homes in all sorts of places on Earth, but if you look at the planet at night from space you can see where most of us live by looking at the lit-up areas.

7 out of 10
of the world's biggest cities are on the coast
=
more than ½
the world's population lives by the sea!

Pacific Ocean

Atlantic Ocean

THE MOST POPULATED CITIES

Tokyo, Japan = **38 million**

Delhi, India = **26 million**

Shanghai, China = **24 million**

Cities with more than **10 million** people are called **MEGACITIES.** MEGA = very big!

HUMANS AT WORK

DEMOGRAPHISTS (deh-mog-rah-fists) are scientists who study populctions. This means they look at how many people there are, where people live, and how this changes over time.

GREENLAND is the BIGGEST island in the world but **LEAST** populated country **(56,000 people).**

Arctic Ocean

JAPAN is DENSELY populated = 3 square metres **PER PERSON.**

9 out of 10 humans live in the Northern Hemisphere.

Indian Ocean

No one lives in the middle of the **SAHARA DESERT!**

Southern Ocean

ANTARCTICA
Loads of penguins
(and a few visiting scientists).

WATER TO DRINK

Humans need water and not just any old water. We need safe, clean water to stay healthy.
Have you ever thought about where your water comes from and how much of it you use each day?

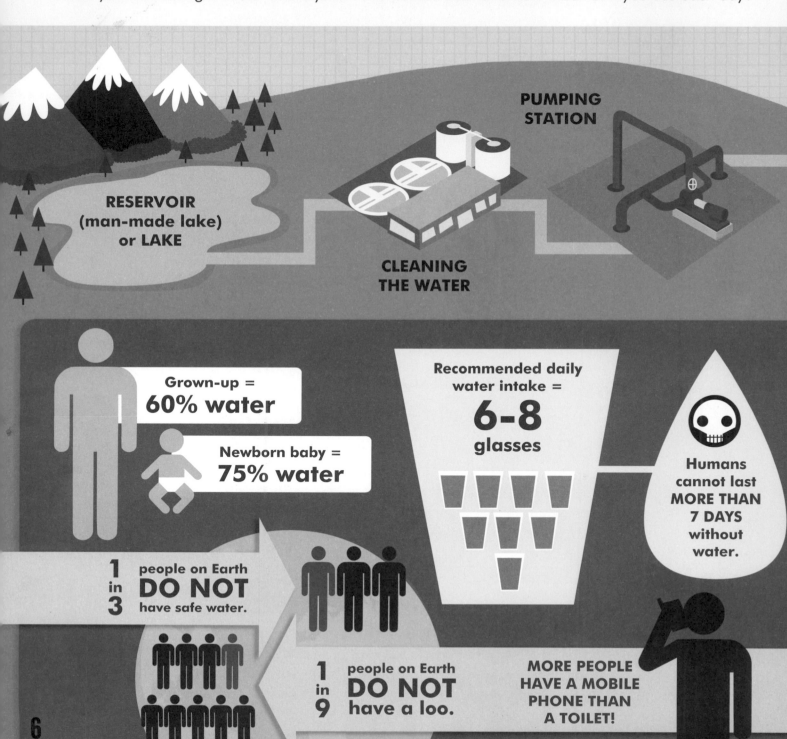

RESERVOIR (man-made lake) or LAKE

CLEANING THE WATER

PUMPING STATION

Grown-up = **60% water**

Newborn baby = **75% water**

Recommended daily water intake = **6-8** glasses

Humans cannot last **MORE THAN 7 DAYS** without water.

1 in 3 people on Earth **DO NOT** have safe water.

1 in 9 people on Earth **DO NOT** have a loo.

MORE PEOPLE HAVE A MOBILE PHONE THAN A TOILET!

HUMANS AT WORK

WATER CONSERVATIONISTS work to protect water supplies in the environment. They help to make sure that water is used carefully. It is too precious to waste!

 = 1 LITRE

60 litres per shower

 1 household flushes **PER YEAR**

 28,000 litres

=

350 BATHFULS

 dripping tap **4 litres** per day

 50 litres per wash

TIPS TO SAVE WATER →

 Fix drips. ✓

 Take shorter showers! ✓

 Could you wear that T-shirt twice? ✓

THE EARTH SHOP

The world is like a giant shop with countries buying and selling different things. These things are called 'resources'. Some resources, like oil and gas, just happen to be in a country already. Other resources, like crops or animals for food, are grown or farmed.

BANANAS

Grown in **hot and tropical** countries.

ECUADOR sells (EXPORTS) ONE THIRD of all the bananas traded in the world.

Picked and packed.

Shipped to Europe in **REEFERS (REFRIGERATED SHIPS)** in **6-12 DAYS.**

TREES

Grown in **cold and northern** parts of the world:

Canada Finland Sweden Russia

Cut down.

Loaded on to trailers.

Transported...

OIL

Found in the **Middle East and Africa:**

**Saudi Arabia
Iraq
Kuwait
Nigeria**

OIL WELL

PIPELINES

TRANSPORTED across the world in tankers.

REFINED = made into petrol, diesel and oil.

STORED

Taken by road tankers and pipelines...

to **PETROL STATIONS.**

to **FACTORIES.**
Made into paints, shampoo, make-up and plastic.

HUMANS AT WORK

An **ECONOMIST** studies the way resources are traded or shared between people and countries. They can help people understand how to make the most of their resources and earn more money.

ETHICAL TRADING

Means that the people working on farms or in factories must be paid enough for their work. It also means that where they work must be safe for them, too.

IMPORT (buying) — is the opposite of — **EXPORT** (selling)

Ripened in warehouses for **4-6 days.**

Trucked to shops.

Bought by consumers.

Eaten!

to timber mills. Made into planks for building.

to papermills. Made into paper.

TIMBER = wood that is made ready to be used for building or carpentry.

Exported all over the world.

4 billion trees are cut down each year to make paper.

60% (two thirds) of all oil taken around the world travels by **TANKER.**

30% (one third) of trading across oceans is **OIL and GAS.**

LARGEST TANKER = **4 million BARRELS of oil** = **636 million litres** (140 million gallons)

Oil is measured in **BARRELS.**

GETTING AROUND

Humans have invented many different ways to travel. We can fly far across the planet in a plane or take to the seas in a ship. We can whiz around on bicycles, motorbikes or in cars. Imagine how long it might take to go right around the world using different forms of transport.

ROAD   RAIL

WATER   AIR

EQUATOR
=
40,070 km
(24,900 miles)

kph = kilometres per hour
mph = miles per hour

HUMANS AT WORK

ENGINEERS use science to solve problems, like how to invent the fastest train. **ASTRONAUTS** are trained to travel into space to do research and explore the Universe.

Earth to Mars = 55 million km (34 million miles)
No human has been there yet!

10 kph (6 mph) TAKES 167 days

100 kph (60 mph) TAKES 17 days

37 kph (23 mph) TAKES 45 days

A ship's speed is measured in KNOTS.

1 KNOT = 1.8 kph (1.15 mph)

100 kph (60 mph) TAKES 17 days

FASTEST TRAIN ON WHEELS

French TGV150

Top Speed = 574 kph (355 mph)

885 kph (550 mph) TAKES under 2 days

AMPHIBIOUS VEHICLES
These can go on land and sea.

TREASURE FROM UNDERGROUND

There are many valuable rocks and minerals under the surface of our planet. Some countries have more of certain kinds of minerals than others. This means they can trade them with other countries.

IRON
is made into steel.

cars   paper clips   beams in skyscrapers

China • Australia • Brazil • USA

COPPER
is easy to bend and stretch.

The average car contains **1.5 km (0.9 miles)** of copper wire.

Chile has 6 out of the 10 LARGEST copper mines in the world.

ORES are rocks that contain metal. We can get that metal out by **HEATING** the rocks.

This is called **SMELTING.**

METAL ORES

TIN
is very light and often mixed with other metals.

China = BIGGEST PRODUCER

COPPER + TIN = BRONZE

PLATINUM
is the **RAREST** and most **EXPENSIVE** metal in the world. It doesn't rust or tarnish.

cars

jewellery

medical instruments

South Africa • Russia

HUMANS AT WORK

METALLURGISTS are scientists who study metals. They can use their knowledge to put different metals together to make strong mixtures called **ALLOYS**. This helps humans make stronger cars and aeroplanes.

DIAMONDS
are beautiful and extremely hard.

jewellery   dentists' drills   drills for oil rigs

Botswana • Russia • Canada

GEMSTONES

RUBIES
Big rubies are rarer than big diamonds.

Burma

SILVER
kills bacteria so it is used in bandages.

jewellery   coins

silver threads in gloves to use with touch-screens

Mexico • Poland • Bolivia

SAPPHIRES

**Kashmir
Burma
Sri Lanka**

EMERALDS

**Colombia
Brazil
Zambia**

GOLD
is shiny, beautiful and super-useful!

It is even used for coating the outside of an astronaut's visor.

China • Australia • USA

PRECIOUS METALS

DEEPEST GOLD MINE
in the world

⬇

SOUTH AFRICA

Mponeng Mine
is nearly
**4 km
(2.5 miles)
deep.**

RUBBISH!

Dumping rubbish and waste on land or in rivers and seas pollutes our world. This then harms people, animals and plants. We only have one planet and we all need to look after it carefully.

We **CHUCK IT** in the **BIN** and **FORGET** about it **BUT...**

PILES OF RUBBISH

There are millions of tonnes of rubbish in landfill.

Some never rots.

Some rots and gives off nasty gases.

This damages the atmosphere.

Plastic in landfill takes **500 YEARS** to rot away (decompose).

PLASTIC IN THE SEA

Plastic dumped in the sea poisons or traps fish and sea animals.

BIGGEST PLASTIC ISLAND

=

Pacific Garbage Patch in Pacific Ocean.

It is **3 x** the size of **France...**

... and weighs same as

500 JUMBO JETS!

This is the same as **250 PIECES** of rubbish for **EVERY PERSON** in the world.

HUMANS AT WORK

PRODUCT DESIGNERS design all the things we use in our lives, from chairs to computers and toothbrushes to schoolbags! Many designers try to make sure that their designs use recycled materials.

TAKE ACTION!

Use your own bags.

Look for unpackaged items.

 Buy refills.

Find out which charities recycle old mobile phones or computers.

Don't buy too much stuff, like food, in the first place!

THINK BEFORE YOU CHUCK IT OUT!
Can it be recycled or reused?

RECYCLING

25 x 2-litre plastic bottles

makes

1 fleece.

1 tonne of **RECYCLED PAPER** saves

17 TREES.

FOOD CANS ARE **100% RECYCLABLE.**

GLASS IS **100% RECYCLABLE.**

Making **1 NEW CAN**

uses the same energy as it takes to

RECYCLE 20 CANS.

COMPOSTING

peelings	**turns kitchen and garden waste into food for plants.**	uncooked veg
old fruit		
teabags		garden cuttings

BURNING RUBBISH

creates energy to power lights and heating... but also harmful gases.

15

TOP INVENTIONS

Humans are really clever and have invented so many wonderful things. It is impossible to choose the best ones, but here is a very small selection. All of them have made a big difference to our lives.

TELEPHONE

When:

1876

Who:

Alexander Graham Bell

Life-changer:

Humans can now talk to people who are not in the same room.

Fun fact:

The first mobile phones were made in the 1970s.

WATERPROOF CLOTHING

When:

1823

Who:

Charles Macintosh

Life-changer:

Humans can keep warm and dry, whatever the weather.

Fun fact:

Raincoats are still sometimes called Mackintoshes or Macs.

PETROL CAR

When:

1885

Who:

Karl Benz

Life-changer:

Humans can now really go places! But...

Fun fact:

Benz's first car only had three wheels!

HUMANS AT WORK

An **INVENTOR** is someone who comes up with an idea for a new gadget or a way of doing things. They can get a special licence to stop other people pinching their ideas! This is called a **PATENT**.

AEROPLANE

When:

1903

Who:

Orville and Wilbur Wright

Life-changer:

Humans can now fly!

Fun fact:

Their first flight = **120 feet (36 metres)** in **12 SECONDS**.

POP-UP TOASTER

When:

1921

Who:

Charles Strite

SLICED BREAD

When:

1928

Who:

Otto Rohwedder

Life-changer:

Human breakfasts are never the same again!

Fun fact:

By 1933 → **8** out of **10** loaves in the USA were **SLICED.**

VACUUM-CLEANER

When:

1901

Who:

Hubert Cecil Booth

Life-changer:

Humans can clean their homes quickly and easily.

Fun fact:

The first vacuum cleaner was called **PUFFING BILLY**. It was so **BIG** it had to be pulled from house to house!

POWER ON THE PLANET

Humans use lots of electricity to power things like lights and machines.
Electricity can be made in many different ways and some of these are better for the planet than others.

ENERGY SOURCES = WAYS TO GET ELECTRICITY

Solar power

is power from the Sun.

Water power

is hydro-electricity.
NO HARMFUL GASES
but dams change the environment near them.

Wind power

turns turbines

to make electricity.

Tidal energy

The tide changes
2 x each day.
Movement of water turns generators

to make electricity.

HARMFUL GAS
=
carbon dioxide (CO$_2$)

greenhouse gas

traps Sun's heat

climate change

Renewable energy → from things that **WILL NOT** run out →

Sun   Wind   Tides   Water

RENEWABLE ENERGY SCIENTISTS work on ways to make electricity from wind, water and sunlight. They have to think about how a wind farm will affect the environment or where is the best place to put solar power 'farms'.

1 kg uranium

makes same amount of energy as

10,000 kg oil

OR

14,000 kg coal

Nuclear energy

is made from a small amount of uranium.

Makes loads of electricity **BUT** also dangerous radioactive waste. **MUST** be stored safely.

Fossil fuels

oil   coal   gas

These make harmful gases when burned.

Biomass energy

is electricity made by burning wood, plants, rubbish. **HARMFUL GASES**

Fracking

releases **FOSSIL FUELS** like gas and oil from shale rock.

It uses **LOADS** of water and may cause **SMALL EARTHQUAKES.**

HARMFUL GASES escape when fuel is burned.

Non-renewable energy → from things that **WILL** run out → Coal Oil Gas Nuclear

CONNECTING THE WORLD

Today it is possible for us to get in touch with almost anyone, anywhere on the planet, immediately! We can also get loads of information at the click of a button. The internet can connect us to the whole wide world!

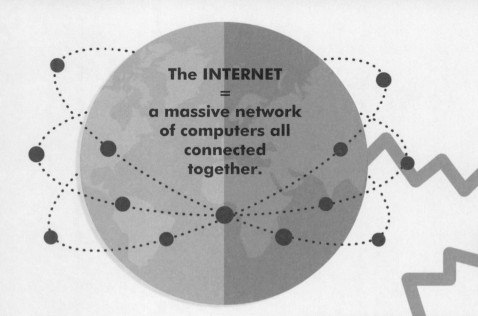

The **INTERNET**
=
a massive network of computers all connected together.

The **WORLD WIDE WEB**
(www or web)
=
loads of WEBPAGES you can look at using the internet.

Your computer's **WEB BROWSER** uses the **INTERNET** to find **WEBPAGES.**

A website is like a book.

Webpages are like chapters inside the book.

The World Wide Web was invented by Sir Tim Berners-Lee in **1989.**

HTML = **Hypertext Markup Language** = the language used for making webpages.

Thanks Tim!

:)

HUMANS AT WORK

COMPUTER PROGRAMMERS tell computers what we want them to do for us. They write code in languages that computers understand. Without programmers there would be no computer games!

STAY SAFE ON-LINE!

Keep all your personal information private.

People you don't know are strangers. They might not be who they say they are.

If you're worried or scared tell a grown-up you trust.

VIDEO CALLING

Talk to family and friends on the other side of the world.

EMAIL

Write to your granny.

BLOGGING

Write a story or poem to share with friends. **BUT ONLY** with people you know and trust.

INSTANT MESSAGING

Send messages to your friends.

HOMEWORK!

Search the web for handy information. **BUT** check website addresses to make sure they are safe and reliable.

21

TALKING TO PEOPLE

Humans are very chatty animals and it is fascinating to think about all the different languages there are in the world. Some languages are spoken more than others. Perhaps you speak some of them yourself?

SPANISH
442 million

HINDI
260 million

JAPANESE
128 million

ENGLISH
378 million

People who speak these as their **FIRST LANGUAGE.**

RUSSIAN
154 million

BENGALI
243 million

HUMANS AT WORK

INTERPRETERS translate the words that someone is saying into a different language. They help people who do not speak the same language as each other to be able to communicate. They often know lots of languages.

There are more than **7,000** languages in the world.

CHINESE
1,299 million

Which language is spoken in the most countries?

ENGLISH
(165 countries)

ARABIC
315 million

Which countries have the most **LIVING** languages?

Nigeria	526
Indonesia	710
Papua New Guinea	841

PORTUGUESE
223 million

ENDANGERED LANGUAGES

151 languages in the world

less than **10 PEOPLE** still speak them.

NO children are learning them

they will soon be **EXTINCT.**

HUMAN WORDS TO KNOW

ALLOY
A metal made by mixing two or more metals together. Copper and tin make bronze.

ARTIFICIAL
means something made by humans. An artificial organ is a copy of the real thing.

ATMOSPHERE
is the air all around Planet Earth.

BILLION
is a thousand million or 1,000,000,000.

CONSUMER
A person who buys things.

DECOMPOSE
means to rot away. Dead things and rubbish decompose.

ENVIRONMENT
is the air, water or land that people and animals live in and on.

EQUATOR
is the imaginary line that runs around the 'waist' of our planet.

ETHICAL
means doing the right thing. An ethical consumer tries to buy things that do not harm the environment or other people.

EXPORT
means to sell to another country or part of the world.

EXTINCT
means completely dead. If a language is extinct it means that no one speaks or writes it any more.

FOSSIL FUELS
are oil, coal and gas. They are natural fuels formed millions of years ago from dead animals and plants.

GENERATE
means to produce or make. Energy sources are used to generate electricity.

HOMO SAPIENS
This is the name given to our own modern human species.

IMPORT
means to buy from another country or part of the world.

LANDFILL
is another word for a rubbish dump or tip.

MEGACITY
A megacity has more than 10 million people living in it.

MIGRATE
means to travel out of your own area to another place.

MINERAL
A valuable or useful substance that has formed naturally under the ground.

NON-RENEWABLE
means that once something is all used up there is no more of it.

ORE
A kind of rock that has useful metal inside it.

POLLUTION
When poisonous or harmful stuff is put into the environment.

POPULATION
is the number of people in a town, country or the world.

PRODUCER
A producer makes or grows things to sell. Producers can be people, companies or whole countries.

RECYCLE
means to reuse something by making it into something else instead of throwing it away.

RENEWABLE
means something that does not run out.

RESOURCE
Something useful that can be used by people or sold for money or exchanged for other resources.

SMELTING
is the way that ores are heated to get the valuable metals out of them.

SOURCE
Where something comes from. The source of nuclear energy is uranium.

TARNISH
is when a shiny metal loses its shine and looks dull and stained.

TRADE
is another word for buying and selling.

TRANSLATE
means to change words into another language.

HELLO!

BONJOUR!